GEO

Ancient Greece

Other books in the Daily Life series:

Ancient Greece

Don Nardo

KIDHAVEN PRESS

THOMSON

---*---
GALE

Detroit • New York • San Diego • San Francisco
Boston • New Haven, Conn. • Waterville, Maine
London • Munich

Picture Credits

Cover photo: Stapleton Collection, UK/Bridgeman Art Library
© Leonard de Selva/CORBIS, 33
DigitalStock, 36
Chris Jouan, 7, 18
© Wolfgang Kaehler/CORBIS, 40
© Erich Lessing/Art Resource, 8, 20, 37
© Massimo Listri/CORBIS, 29
© North Wind Pictures, 10, 11, 16, 23, 24, 30
© Gianni Dagli Orti/CORBIS, 14, 25
Réunion des Musées Nationaux/Art Resource, 19, 38
© Scala/Art Resource, 27, 34
© Stock Montage, Inc., 12

Library of Congress Cataloging-in-Publication Data

Nardo, Don, 1947–
  Ancient Greece / by Don Nardo.
    p. cm. — (Daily life)
Summary: Discusses the daily life of ancient Greeks including
citizenship, the household, athletics, and religion.
    ISBN 0-7377-0956-1
    1. Greece—Civilization—To 146 B.C.—Juvenile literature.
[1. Greece—Civilization—To 146 B.C.— 2. Greece—History—
To 146 B.C.] I. Title. II. Series.
    DF77 .N372 2002
    938—dc21

2001001438

Contents

CHAPTER ONE

Citizenship in a Greek City-State

A ncient Greece was never a unified nation. Instead, it was made up of hundreds of **city-states**. A city-state was a tiny country built around a central town. Usually (but not always), such a town grew up around a steep hill. That hill was called an **acropolis**, meaning "the city's high place" in Greek. The people retreated there in times of danger. Each town had a marketplace, called an agora. Farmers from the surrounding countryside came to the agora to sell their crops.

Most Greek city-states were small, with populations of ten thousand or fewer people each. Nevertheless, each state viewed itself as a separate nation with its own proud traditions. And its members developed its own laws, type of government, and other institutions. So everyday life sometimes differed considerably from one Greek city to another.

Still, Greeks everywhere had a few basic things in common. First, they all spoke Greek; so people from various city-states could easily communicate, conduct trade, and read one another's literature. They also worshiped the same gods.

Ancient Greece

Today, historians know much more about the things all Greeks had in common than about their differences. That is because the evidence of life in most Greek city-states has disappeared over the centuries. The major exception is Athens. Most of the surviving firsthand information about Greek civilization comes from Athenian writers and describes Athenian history, customs, and ideas. Athens was the largest, most populous, and most prosperous city. So it was not an average Greek city. Nevertheless, scholars feel that life in ancient Athens was similar in most ways to life in other parts of ancient Greece.

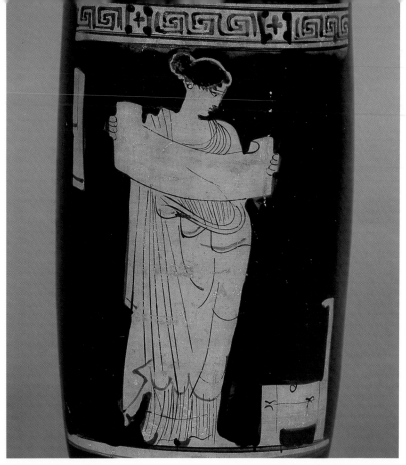

A painted vase shows a woman reading from a scroll. Greeks everywhere spoke and wrote the same language.

The People Decide

One factor that did set Athens apart from other Greek cities, at least for a while, was its political system. Athens was the first city in the world to institute **democracy**. This was very unusual at the time. (Athenian democracy began in 508 B.C., at about the beginning of what historians call Greece's Classical Age, which lasted until 323 B.C.) After a while, some other Greek cities came to admire Athenian democracy. And a number of them adopted similar democratic governments.

In a democracy, of course, the people decide how the government should be run. In Athens and other Greek democracies, citizens met on a regular basis to discuss how the community should operate. Such a meeting was known as an **assembly**. Members of the Athenian assembly voted to elect public officials. They also had the authority to declare war, make peace, grant citizenship, and establish colonies. The assembly even had the power to tell the generals what strategy to use in waging war.

The Athenian assembly met outside, on the city's Pnyx Hill. First, a herald called for silence. Next, a priest said a prayer aloud and killed a pig as an offering to the gods. Then the herald asked who wanted to speak. One at a time, citizens addressed the crowd. The listeners applauded those they agreed with and booed or hissed those they disagreed with.

Evidence suggests that in the Classical Age, attendance at the Athenian assembly averaged between four thousand and six thousand. If too few citizens showed up, a group of specially trained slaves chased other citizens through the streets. The slaves swatted the citizens' clothes with a rope dipped in red paint. Any man caught with a red stain on his tunic had to pay a fine.

A Fair Justice System

Another important aspect of Athenian democracy was its fair justice system. A typical jury in a court case numbered four or five hundred members. Because of the large number, it was almost impossible for someone to use threats or bribes to influence the jury.

A group of Athenian jurors discuss the merits of a case.

Athenian courts operated differently than those in modern democracies. First, there was no judge. Also, the cases were not tried by lawyers. Instead, the litigants (those accusing someone or defending themselves) pled their own cases before the jury. The litigants also had to gather their own evidence and witnesses. Any male citizen could take a case to court.

Citizens Versus Foreigners

The fact that only male citizens could take a case to court shows that the Athenians defined the term citizen rather narrowly. Only free males born in Athenian territory enjoyed complete citizenship rights. These included the rights to vote and hold public office. Female

Athenians were citizens, too. But they belonged to a special type, the *astai*—those without political rights.

Another class of Athenians, called **metics**, also lacked political rights. *Metics* were foreigners—either non-Greeks or Greeks from other cities—who lived and worked in Athens. They were mostly merchants and tradesmen such as potters, metalworkers, and jewelers. Not only were *metics* barred from taking part in government, they also could not own land.

Thus, full citizenship was a special and cherished right in Athens and other Greek cities. Loss of citizenship,

Discussions about politics, philosophy, and other subjects commonly took place on the streets of Athens.

Slave girls talk while drawing water from a public fountain. Most Athenian slaves were well treated.

called **atimia**, was highly dreaded. An **atimos**, a man who had lost his citizenship, could not speak in the assembly or law courts. Neither could he hold public office or enter a temple or the marketplace. Moreover, any citizen who saw an **atimos** in one of these areas was allowed to arrest him on the spot.

Slavery a Natural Fact of Life

At least an **atimos** had earlier been a citizen and knew what it felt like to have rights. In contrast, slaves had no rights at all. Most Greek slaves were the children of other slaves or had been captured during wars. They did most of the manual labor in society; that left many citizens free to pursue politics, the arts, and other endeavors. In the Classical Age, Athens had perhaps one hundred thousand slaves, about a third of the total population. An average family probably had two or three slaves, while a well-to-do citizen kept fifteen to twenty. Various craft shops had even more slaves. An Athenian **metic** named Cephalus used about 120 slaves in his shieldmaking shop.

For the most part, Greek slaves were well treated. Often they became trusted members of the families that owned them. Most also received small wages. They could either spend this money or save it; a few saved enough to buy their freedom. By contrast, the minority of slaves who toiled in mines earned no wages and could not buy their freedom. They were chained day and night and often treated brutally. Working in Athens's famous silver mines was seen as a death sentence.

Modern societies view slavery as immoral, even evil. The Greeks, however, like other ancient peoples,

A model of the Acropolis. Its temples filled all Athenians, free and slave alike, with pride.

accepted it as the will of the gods and a natural fact of life. According to the noted Athenian thinker Aristotle:

> A human being who by nature belongs to another . . . is by nature a slave. One person belongs to another if . . . he is an article of property. . . . There is only a slight difference between the services rendered by slaves and by animals; both give assistance with their bodies.[1]

Slavery shaped and affected Greek society at all levels. This alone made ancient Greek life very different from life today.

CHAPTER TWO

The Family and Household

A s remains true today, in ancient Greece the most basic social unit was the family. The Greeks called the family the *oikos*. It included not only parents and children, but also grandparents and other relatives, and all property, including land and slaves.

Whether in the countryside or town, the family and the home it occupied were the main focus of Greek life. The father was head of the household and his word was law. He made and enforced the rules, distributed money to family members, bought slaves, and arranged for his children's education. His wife, children, other live-in relatives, and slaves each had their own duties. In a way, then, the home was like a smaller version of a city-state. In each case a number of people worked together under central leadership for the good of all. The famous Greek thinker Plato recognized this fact, writing, "A large household may be compared to a small state."[2]

Women's Duties

Even though men were in charge of their homes, very few spent much time in them. In Athens, for example, outdoor work occupied most of a farmer's day; and

Only the very rich could afford the lavish lifestyle pictured here.

townsmen were most often found in the marketplace, the law courts, or the gym. "I certainly do not pass my time indoors," says a well-to-do man in a book by the Athenian writer Xenophon. "My wife is quite capable of looking after the house by herself."[3]

This remark captures an important reality of Athenian life. A man's wife (or mother or other female relative if he was not married) actually ran the household from day to day. Many Athenian women spent a majority of their time at home. But most did not feel confined or bored. Within the home, women had many and varied duties, all of which were essential to the success of the household. These included making clothes, helping to prepare meals, overseeing the children and servants, paying the bills, and keeping the home clean and well organized.

Houses and Their Contents

Most of the Athenian homes that the men owned and the women managed were simple in design. They were also smaller and more modestly furnished than the average modern house. Athenian houses usually featured stone foundations and walls made of sun-dried clay bricks. The bricks were sometimes strengthened with wooden timbers; still, they began to crumble after a few years, forcing owners to make frequent repairs. In poorer homes, especially in the countryside, the floors consisted of hard-beaten earth. People often covered the bare earth with straw mats, layers of pebbles, or flagstones. Roofs were most often made of baked pottery tiles.

Like houses in other parts of Greece, the average Athenian house was built around a central courtyard. This area was roofless to take advantage of natural lighting. Some courtyards had wells to provide a ready water supply. And most, if not all, had small altars

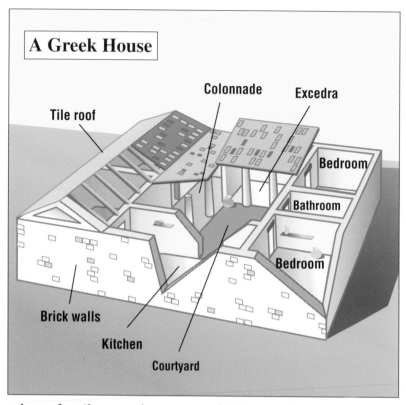

A Greek House

Colonnade

Excedra

Tile roof

Bedroom

Bathroom

Brick walls

Bedroom

Kitchen

Courtyard

where family members prayed. Houses in towns generally had small courtyards, while in the country, nicer homes, called villas, had bigger courtyards and large gardens.

Lining the central courtyard were various rooms, most of them small. These included the exedra, a sitting area with one side open to the inner courtyard; the kitchen, which had an open **hearth** for cooking and tables for food preparation; and a few bedrooms.

The lighting and heating of these rooms was primitive by today's standards. Oil lamps and candles were the chief lighting devices. Heat was provided by the household hearths and also by **braziers**, metal containers that burned charcoal.

The average home also had a bathroom. It commonly contained a tub, slightly smaller than modern versions, made of **terra-cotta** (baked clay). Usually, the family slaves used buckets to fill the tub. A few of the richer homes may have featured showers, with water carried into the home by clay pipes. Many Athenian bathrooms had terra-cotta toilets as well; but in homes without toilets, it was necessary to use a pot, which had to be emptied by hand.

Entertaining Guests

Well-to-do Athenian houses had, in addition, a special room called an *andron*. Here the head of the household held banquets. He also entertained his male guests in after-dinner parties called **symposia**. During the preliminary meal, served by slaves, the men reclined on

Slaves serve the male guests at a banquet in a well-to-do Athenian home.

couches. Afterward, the host and his guests drank wine, chatted, told stories and riddles, sang songs, and/or played games.

One of the most popular party games was *cottabos.* The players tried to flip the wine from their cups into a bowl or vase or at a target drawn on the wall. In addition, the host might bring in entertainers. These included flute players and other musicians as well as dancers and acrobats.

The household women were not allowed to attend such gatherings. According to custom, it was improper for the women to mix socially with men from outside the family. So when the father entertained guests, the women retired to a special room (or rooms) in the rear of the house. It was called the "women's quarters." A Roman writer named Cornelius Nepos visited Athens not long after the Classical Age. He found this separation of men and women strange. (Roman women were not nearly as sheltered as Athenian women.) "What Roman would blush to take his wife to a dinner party?" Nepos asked. He continues:

Painted pottery shows women relaxing in the "women's quarters."

It is very different in Athens; for there the woman [of the house] is not admitted to a dinner party, unless relatives only are present. And she keeps to the . . . part of the house called the "women's apartment," that no man can enter who is not near of kin.[4]

Young Children

Children were also forbidden to attend their father's banquets and parties unless they were family affairs. Athenian children were almost always born in the home. All female members of the household, including slaves, helped with the delivery. The family celebrated the birth when the baby was five days old. Friends and relatives sent gifts (customary favorite delicacies being octopus or squid), and sometimes the parents announced the child's name at that time. Those families that could afford it held a second ceremony five days later. If so, they waited until then to name the baby.

As the children grew they played with toys familiar to modern children. Among these were balls, dolls, tops, yo-yos, and toy carts and chariots (similar to today's toy cars and trucks). At age seven, young boys began going to school, so they were away from home for part of the day. (In contrast, girls stayed home and learned weaving and other household arts from their mothers.) Some fathers had a household slave escort their sons to school to make sure they behaved there. Thus, slaves and children along with free adult men and women played their expected roles in the family and household.

CHAPTER THREE

Sports Training and Competition

A ll Greeks had an interest in a wide variety of athletic games and sports. In fact, formal, organized sports contests in the modern sense originated in ancient Greece. Many Greeks came to believe in what they called the "physical and mental ideal." The idea was to become a "complete" person by developing a keen mind in a strong, athletic body. The wide acceptance of this concept is illustrated by a common adage the Greeks coined to describe a backward person: "He can neither read nor swim."[5]

Athletics and physical training were so important in ancient Greek life that many institutions were developed to promote them. In the Classical Age almost every Greek town had a gym and a wrestling school (large towns like Athens had several). Daily exercise and other forms of informal athletic activities took place in these facilities as well as in fields or on the streets.

Also, numerous formal athletic competitions grew up all across Greece. Some were at the local level, as nearly every Greek town staged its own yearly games. A few athletic games had wider appeal. According to tra-

Greek athletes work out in a gymnasium. Athletes often trained and competed in the nude.

dition, in 776 B.C. the first Olympic Games were held. They honored Zeus, ruler of the gods. These famous contests took place every four years at Olympia (in the city-state of Elis, in southern Greece). The Olympics were **panhellenic**, meaning "all-Greek," because they drew people from all over the Greek world. Three other major panhellenic games developed. One was the Pythian Games, honoring Apollo, god of prophecy. The Pythian Games were held at Apollo's sacred shrine at Delphi (in central Greece). The other two were the Isthmian Games, honoring Poseidon, god of the seas, and

Men compete in the "race in armor" at an Athens athletic competition.

the Nemean Games, dedicated to Zeus. These "big four" games, like the Greek language and religious worship, helped bind all Greeks together in a common culture.

Informal Athletic Activities

On the local level, a typical gym in a Greek town had several useful features. These included rooms for changing, bathing, and socializing. Each gym also had a small field for practicing various outdoor sports. And in keeping with the physical-mental ideal, most gyms had small libraries, reading rooms, and/or lecture halls dedicated to higher learning.

Another place Greek men went to keep fit was the *palaestra*, or wrestling school. Wrestling training was the most important aspect of boys' physical education.

Young men often wrestled informally, much as modern young men play sandlot football and baseball. Also, Greek society expected that adult males would enjoy and participate in wrestling as much as they would discussing politics with their friends.

Other informal sports activities included fishing, boating, and ballplaying. One ball game the Greeks played was *episkyros*. A team sport, it appears to have been similar to modern rugby. Greek men also enjoyed swimming. Several ancient Greek writers mentioned how the ability to swim came in handy. One was the fifth-century B.C. historian Herodotus. In his description of the sea battle of Salamis (fought against the Persians in 480 B.C.), he wrote:

This Greek ball game played with bent sticks may have been similar to modern field hockey.

Most of the Greeks could swim, and those who lost their ships . . . swam over to [the island of] Salamis. Most of the enemy, on the other hand, being unable to swim, were drowned.[6]

Hunting was also a popular Greek pastime, especially among members of the upper classes. They could best afford horses and packs of hunting hounds, which were expensive. The most common kinds of animals they hunted were wild boar, bears, fox, deer, rabbits, and birds.

Formal Athletic Contests

Formal athletic contests were also very popular at the local level. Because Athens was the largest and most prosperous Greek city, its games became particularly famous and admired. They were part of a religious festival known as the Panathenaea. Events included both short and long footraces; a footrace in which the runners wore armor; throwing the discus and javelin; the broad jump; wrestling, boxing, and the *pankration* (a brutal combination of wrestling, boxing, and street-fighting); and horse and chariot races.

The "big four" competitions, including the Olympics, featured these same events. In Athens, as in other Greek towns, free males of all walks of life regularly trained for and competed in these major games. (Women and slaves were excluded. However, women were eventually allowed to take part in their own small, separate games. Called the Heraea because they honored the goddess Hera, Zeus's wife, they took place at

A Roman copy of the Discus Thrower, carved by an Athenian sculptor about 450 B.C.

Olympia every four years. There was only one event—a footrace of about 525 feet.)

Of the four major games, the Olympics was the most important. Every four years the men who had trained for it eagerly awaited the arrival of the "truce-bearers." These three heralds visited every Greek city and invited all men to attend. The heralds also announced the sacred Olympic truce. For three months, all participating cities could not make war or impose death penalties. This ensured safe passage for the thousands of athletes, spectators, and religious pilgrims who attended the games.

When they reached Olympia, these travelers found an impressive array of buildings, shrines, and athletic facilities. Among them were temples dedicated to Zeus and other gods. (The giant statue of Zeus that sat in his temple made the list of the Seven Wonders of the ancient world.) In addition, Olympia featured eleven storehouses that held gold and other offerings to the gods; a stadium for running, jumping, and throwing events; a track for horse and chariot races; a large gym; and several public baths. There was also a small hotel for important officials and visiting royalty. The rest of the fifty to sixty thousand visitors slept in tents or under the stars.

Rewards for the Winners

The only prize directly awarded at Olympia was a crown of leaves. However, Olympic and other "big four" winners received substantial rewards when they returned home. The Athenian government paid an

An Etruscan vase painting shows Greek youths competing in a foot race.

Olympic victor five hundred drachmas, for instance. (The average Greek worker earned about one drachma per day, or three hundred drachmas per year, in the late fifth century B.C. So an athlete could get more than a year and a half's salary by winning a single footrace!)

In addition to cash prizes, winning athletes received valuable objects they could sell at a profit. Among these were gold or silver cups and large jars of olive oil.

A winning athlete is crowned with a wreath of laurel leaves.

The olive oil awarded to each winner was worth up to twelve hundred drachmas, enough to buy two or three houses in Athens. In that city, men who had won events in the "big four" games received free meals for life. A surviving inscription reads: "All those who have won an athletic event at the Olympic, Pythian, Isthmian, or Nemean games shall have the right to eat free of charge in the city hall."[7]

Finally, successful athletes enjoyed enormous fame and respect. Poets composed songs about them. And sculptors carved statues of them made of bronze or stone. In this way some victors became, in a sense, immortal. And the modern world gained a model to copy in creating its own athletic games. Today, high school, college, and Olympic athletes compete in many of the same events that the Greeks perfected and glorified almost three thousand years ago.

CHAPTER FOUR

Religion and Worship

Religion played an extremely important role in ancient Greek life. Some kind of religious ritual accompanied nearly every gathering or important occasion, private or public. No pious Greek ate a meal, for example, without offering a portion of the food to the gods. All major life cycle events, such as birth, marriage, and death, featured religious ceremonies, too. In addition, military generals made an offering to the gods before battle, and public meetings, such as those of Athens's assembly, began with offerings and prayers.

Today religion is viewed largely as a private affair. By contrast, the Greeks saw it also as a public concern. Greeks everywhere felt it was essential to a community's welfare to maintain the goodwill of the gods. If one person offended the gods, it might bring down their wrath on the whole community. Moreover, most Greeks made a connection between religion and patriotism. They believed that certain gods favored certain cities above other cities. Each city had its personal **patron** god, therefore, who watched over and protected that community. Athens's patron was Athena, goddess of war and wisdom. The goddess Hera protected the

This fanciful modern painting shows Athenian citizens inside the Parthenon.

city of Argos. And Poseidon was the patron god of Corinth.

Not surprisingly, such divine favors did not come free. Rather, the gods expected something in return. The most common view was that they would provide good fortune, prosperity, and safety as long as the people did certain things. First, they had to uphold their oaths, which they made in the gods' names. Second, they had to make the proper prayers and offerings. People were also expected to celebrate the traditional religious festivals faithfully. And they consulted the gods directly

The sea god Poseidon stands over one of his symbols—the dolphin—in this ancient sculpture.

in times of uncertainty or crisis; this was done through **oracles**, female priests who conveyed the gods' words to humans.

The Olympian Gods

The gods the Greeks worshiped had human form and personalities. They got married, had children, fought among themselves, and sometimes made mistakes. One important factor separated them from people, however. That was their tremendous power. The gods could alter nature or destroy humans and their cities at will. So people had no choice but to recognize and respect the power wielded by the gods.

The major gods were known as the "Olympians." The title derived from early traditions claiming that they dwelled atop Mount Olympus (in northern Greece), the tallest mountain in the land. The Olympian gods included Zeus, Hera, Poseidon, Apollo, Athena, and several others. According to legend, they had overthrown an earlier race of gods, the Titans, in a great battle in the remote past. And one of the Titans—Prometheus—had fashioned the human race from mud and clay.

Temples and Sanctuaries

Prometheus instructed humans about the proper forms of worshiping the gods. The most visible examples of this worship were temples dedicated to these deities. At first the temples were small and made of wood. By the beginning of the Classical Age, however, they were much larger and made of stone. The most beautiful and famous Greek temple was (and remains) the Parthenon. The Athenians built it atop the Acropolis in the 440s B.C. to honor their patron, Athena.

The Greeks believed that Athena and other gods actually lived from time to time inside their temples. So these structures were seen as sacred places. The surrounding grounds, where the altars stood and worship took place, were also sacred. To respect a god's privacy, no worship took place inside a temple, as it does in modern churches. Together, a temple and its grounds made up a god's sacred sanctuary.

The ruins of the Parthenon stand at the summit of the Acropolis in Athens.

Religious Festivals and Sacrifice

These sanctuaries naturally became the focus of the religious festivals. For example, Athens's largest festival—the Panathenaea (meaning "all the Athenians")—centered on the Erechtheum. This temple and its sanctuary were located on the Athenian Acropolis not far from the Parthenon. The Erechtheum housed Athena's sacred wooden statue. Legend said that it had fallen there from the sky untold ages before.

The Panathenaea began with a parade of thousands of worshipers. They marched through the city streets carrying Athena's sacred robe. Each year a group of specially chosen young maidens wove a new robe for the goddess. The goal was to bring the new robe to the Erechtheum and drape it around the sacred wooden statue.

When the worshipers climbed the Acropolis and reached the Erechtheum, they first took part in a large-scale public offering to Athena. Such offerings were called sacrifices. First, the worshipers draped flower garlands over a cow, sheep, or other animal and led it to the altar. Next, a male or female priest poured water

Young people carry water jars in a famous Parthenon carving.

over the altar to purify it. Then the priest used a club to stun the animal and a knife to cut its throat. The blood drained into a bowl. Finally, several priests used axes and knives to slaughter the animal. The bones and organs were wrapped in the fat and burned, generating smoke, which rose up to nourish and appease the goddess. Meanwhile, the worshipers divided, cooked, and ate the meat.

After the sacrifices, the worshipers in the Panathenaea held a solemn ceremony in which they presented the sacred robe to Athena. Later, in a separate

In this painting on a cup, two Greek men are about to sacrifice a pig.

ritual, some young women removed the old robe, washed the statue, and put on the new robe. The Athenians believed that performing all of these steps would please the goddess and thereby benefit their city.

Prayer and the Afterlife

Another way the Greeks pleased the gods was through prayer. People said prayers at births and marriages, before traveling, at funerals and public meetings, and on many other occasions. A Greek prayed standing, with hands raised, palm upward. Kneeling in prayer, which is common today, was seen as unworthy of a free person. Also, people usually said prayers aloud unless they had some special reason to conceal them.

Many people today pray, and they can easily identify with this aspect of ancient Greek worship. However, certain other aspects of Greek religion set it apart from most modern faiths. For example, the Greeks had no sacred text like the Christian Bible, the Jewish Torah, or the Muslim Koran.

Neither did the Greeks have any universally accepted concepts of the afterlife. Rather, these beliefs varied widely. A common early concept was that Hermes, the messenger god, guided the soul into the Underworld, the realm of the dead. This was a sad and dismal place. Most souls in the Underworld wandered aimlessly around a large, sunless plain. By contrast, some Greeks concluded that the soul did not survive after death. They thought that when people died, their thoughts and energy floated away into the sky and dissolved.

The messenger god, Hermes, guided people's spirits to the Underworld.

Many Greeks came to reject these cheerless, rather grim views of life after death. Some turned to religious groups that promised to reveal the secrets of enjoying a happy afterlife. These groups were known as "mystery" cults. The name came from the fact that most of the ceremonies were kept secret. The most famous Greek mystery cult was the Eleusinian Mysteries, centered at Eleusis, twelve miles west of Athens. Members worshiped Demeter, the goddess who oversaw agriculture. They believed that when they died they would go to a comfortable, sunny place and live there forever.

Though beliefs about the afterlife differed, nearly all Greeks agreed on the importance of certain core beliefs and rituals. Most important, the gods had to be appeased through public sacrifice and prayer. As Xenophon put it: "All things in every place are in the hands of the gods, [and] they . . . rule all things."[8]

Notes

Chapter 1: Citizenship in a Greek City-State

1. Aristotle, *Politics,* in Renford Bambrough, ed., *The Philosophy of Aristotle.* New York: New American Library, 1963, pp. 387–88.

Chapter 2: The Family and Household

2. Plato, *Statesman,* in *The Dialogues of Plato,* trans. Benjamin Jowett. Chicago: Encyclopaedia Britannica, 1952, p. 581.

3. Quoted in Xenophon, *Oeconomicus,* in *Xenophon: Memorabilia and Oeconomicus,* trans. E.C. Marchant. Cambridge, MA: Harvard University Press, 1965, p. 415.

4. Cornelius Nepos, *The Book of the Great Generals of Foreign Nations,* trans. John Rolfe. Cambridge, MA: Harvard University Press, 1960, p. 371.

Chapter 3: Sports Training and Competition

5. Plato, *Laws,* in *The Dialogues of Plato,* p. 670. Several Greek writers mentioned this adage.

6. Herodotus, *The Histories,* trans. Aubrey de Sélincourt. New York: Penguin Books, 1972, p. 553.

7. Quoted in Waldo E. Sweet, ed., *Sport and Recreation in Ancient Greece: A Sourcebook with Translations.* New York: Oxford Univeristy Press, 1987, p. 120.

Chapter 4: Religion and Worship

8. Xenophon, *Anabasis,* trans. W.H.D. Rouse. New York: New American Library, 1959, p. 57.

Glossary

acropolis: "The city's high place"; a central hill around which many Greek towns were built. The capitalized version—Acropolis—refers to the one in Athens.

assembly: A meeting in which local citizens discussed and debated issues and/or voted for leaders.

astai: Citizens who lacked political rights; the term most often referred to women.

atimia: Loss of citizenship. One who suffered such a loss was called an *atimos*.

brazier: A metal container that burned charcoal.

city-state: A small nation built around a central town.

democracy: A form of government in which the people vote for their leaders.

hearth: A fireplace or open oven.

metics: Foreigners living in Athens. They had no political rights.

oikos: The family. (The plural is *oikoi*.)

oracle: A message thought to come from the gods; or the sacred site where such a message was given; or the female priest who delivered the message.

palaestra: A wrestling school or facility.

panhellenic: "All-Greek"; a term used to describe ideas or events common to most or all Greek states.

patron: A god or goddess thought to provide special protection to a city.

symposium: An after-dinner party. (The plural is symposia.)

terra-cotta: Baked clay.

For Further Exploration

Isaac Azimov, *The Greeks: A Great Adventure*. Boston: Houghton Mifflin, 1965. An excellent, entertaining overview of Greek history and culture.

David Bellingham, *An Introduction to Greek Mythology*. Secaucus, NJ: Chartwell Books, 1989. Explains the major Greek myths and legends and their importance to the ancient Greeks. Contains many beautiful photos and drawings.

Peter Connolly, *The Greek Armies*. Morristown, NJ: Silver Burdette, 1979. A fine, detailed study of Greek armor, weapons, and battle tactics, filled with colorful, accurate illustrations. Highly recommended.

Denise Dersin, *Greece: Temples, Tombs, and Treasures*. Alexandria, VA: Time-Life Books, 1994. This handsome volume has an excellent, up-to-date, and beautifully illustrated chapter on Athens's golden age.

Don Nardo, *Greek and Roman Theater*. San Diego: Lucent Books, 1995; *The Age of Pericles*. San Diego: Lucent Books, 1996; *The Parthenon*. San Diego: Lucent Books, 1999; *Greek and Roman Sport*. San Diego: Lucent Books, 1999; *Life in Ancient Athens*. San Diego: Lucent Books, 2000; *The Ancient Greeks*. San Diego: Lucent Books, 2001. These books, which are aimed at junior high school readers, provide a great deal of information about ancient Greek history and culture.

Susan Peach and Anne Millard, *The Greeks.* London: Usborne, 1990. A general overview of the history, culture, myths, and everyday life of ancient Greece, presented in a format suitable to young, basic readers.

Jonathan Rutland, *See Inside an Ancient Greek Town.* New York: Barnes & Noble, 1995. This colorful introduction to ancient Greek life is aimed at basic readers.

Index